Bond

Third papers

9–10 years

Michellejoy Hughes

Comprehension

Nelson Thornes

Published in 2009 by:
Nelson Thornes Ltd
Delta Place
27 Bath Road
CHELTENHAM
GL53 7TH
United Kingdom

10 11 12 13 / 10 9 8 7 6 5 4 3

A catalogue record for this book is available from the British Library

ISBN 978 1 4085 0400 0

Illustrations by Angela Knowles
Page make-up by Pantek Arts Ltd, Maidstone, Kent

Printed and bound in Egypt by Sahara Printing Company

Acknowledgements

Extract from *Alice's Adventures in Wonderland* by Lewis Carroll sourced from www.gutenberg.org; Extract from *Swiss Family Robinson* by J.D.Wyss sourced from www.childrensnursery.org.uk; Extract from *The Counties of England* (Derbyshire) by Charlotte Mason sourced from www.mainlesson.com; Extract from *From a Railway Carriage* by Robert Louis Stevenson sourced from www.oldpoetry.com; Extract from *The Story of England* (Britain and the Britons) by Samuel B Harding sourced from www.mainlesson.com; Extract from *'Twas the Night before Christmas* by Clement C Moore sourced from www.gutenberg.org.

Before you get started

About Bond

Bond is the leading name in practice for 11+ and other selective school exams (e.g. 7+, 12+, 13+, CEE), as well as for general practice in key learning skills. The series provides resources across the 5–13 years age range for English and maths and 6–12 years for verbal reasoning and non-verbal reasoning. Bond's English resources are also ideal preparation for teacher assessments at Key Stages 1 and 3, as well as for Key Stage 2 SATs.

About comprehension

Comprehension is a vital life skill. It involves the ability to critically read and understand written material and then to take or use relevant information from it. This skill is developed in children from an early age; consequently comprehension exercises form a core component of most English exams and assessments in school.

To test the breadth of a child's comprehension ability, exams may present one or more extracts taken from works of fiction (i.e. novels), poetry, playscripts or non-fiction (i.e. biographies, leaflets, advertisements, newspaper and magazine articles). Questions are likely to range from those that require direct, literal answers (e.g. 'What colour was the girl's coat?') to those that, with increasing levels of complexity, involve inferring information and offering a personal opinion (e.g. 'Why did Tom decide to put the money back?'; 'How do you think he felt when he realised that the money had gone?').

Children are likely to face a range of different comprehension tasks throughout Key Stages 1–3, particularly in English end-of-year assessments, Key Stage 2 SATs and 11+ (as well as other selective) English exams. Both wide reading and regular, focused comprehension practice are therefore essential for success.

What does the book contain?

- **10 papers** – providing comprehension practice in fiction, non-fiction and poetry. Each test includes one or more passages to read, followed by questions. The number of questions in a paper may vary but each test is worth a total of 35 marks. The comprehension texts and questions have been pitched at the level of a typical 11+ exam.

- **Tutorial links** throughout – 📖 – this icon appears in the margin next to the questions. It indicates links to the relevant sections in *The secrets of Comprehension*, our invaluable guide that explains all key aspects of comprehension.

- **Scoring devices** – there are score boxes in the margins and a Progress Chart on page 48.

- **Answers** – located in an easily-removed central pull-out section. If you lose your answers, please email cservices@nelsonthornes.com for another copy.

How can you use this book?

Flexibility is one of the great strengths of the Bond series. These comprehension books can therefore be used at home, in school and by tutors to:

- set timed exercises – for each paper allow around 10 minutes to read the extract(s), followed by 30 minutes to answer the questions; this will provide good practice for 11+ (and other exam) time frames
- provide regular, bite-sized practice
- highlight strengths and weaknesses
- identify individual needs
- set homework
- help build a complete 11+ English preparation strategy alongside other Bond resources (see below).

It is best to start at the beginning and work through the papers in order. If you are using the book as part of a careful 11+ preparation plan, we suggest that you also have these other Bond resources close at hand:

The secrets of Comprehension: this practical handbook is an essential support for *Bond Comprehension 9–10 years*. *The secrets of Comprehension* clearly explains to children how to read and understand a text, how to approach the core question types and how to assess their own answers. The margin icons in *Bond Comprehension 9–10 years* indicate which questions are cross-referenced to the relevant sections of this handbook.

Bond Assessment Papers in English: these graded books provide lots of timed practice at comprehension, spelling, grammar and vocabulary work, in line with the scope of 11+ (and other) English exams.

How to do … 11+ English: the subject guide that explains all aspects of 11+ English.

The Parents' Guide to the 11+: the step-by-step guide to the whole 11+ experience. It clearly explains the 11+ process, provides guidance on how to assess a child and helps you to set a complete action plan for a strategic run-in to the exam.

See the inside front cover for more details of these books.

What does a child's score mean and how can it be improved?

It is unfortunately impossible to guarantee that a child will pass the 11+ English exam (or any comprehension test) if they achieve a certain score on a practice paper. Success on the day will depend on a host of factors, including the performance of the other children. However, we can give some guidance on what a score indicates and how to improve it.

If children colour in the Progress Chart (page 48), this will give an indication of performance in percentage terms. The Next Steps Planner inside the back cover will then help you to decide what to do next. It is always valuable to go over incorrect answers with children. If they are having trouble with any particular question type, follow the tutorial links to *The secrets of Comprehension* for step-by-step explanations and further practice.

Don't forget the website…!

Visit www.bond11plus.co.uk for lots of free resources, advice and information about Bond, the 11+ and helping children to do their best.

Key words

adjective	a word that describes somebody or something
alliteration	a repetition of the same sound *five funny frogs*
collective noun	a word referring to a group *swarm*
conjunction	a word used to link sentences, phrases or words *and, but*
grammar rule	a rule that we apply to make a word when adding a prefix or suffix, e.g. reply – take off the y and add 'ies' to make *replies*
homophone	a word that has the same sound as another but a different meaning or spelling *right/write*
metaphor	an expression in which something is described in terms usually associated with another *the sky is a <u>sapphire sea</u>*
monologue	a long speech given by one person
narrator	a person who is telling a story
noun	a word for somebody or something
preposition	a word that relates other words to each other *he sat <u>behind</u> me the book <u>on</u> the table*
pronoun	a word used to replace a noun
simile	an expression to describe what something is like *as cold as ice*
verb	a 'doing' or 'being' word

Alice was beginning to get very tired of sitting by her sister on the bank, and of having nothing to do. Once or twice she had peeped into the book her sister was reading, but it had no pictures or conversations in it, "and what is the use of a book," thought Alice, "without pictures or conversations?"

So she was considering in her own mind (as well as she could, for the day made her feel very sleepy and stupid), whether the pleasure of making a daisy-chain would be worth the trouble of getting up and picking the daisies, when suddenly a White Rabbit with pink eyes ran close by her.

There was nothing so very remarkable in that, nor did Alice think it so very much out of the way to hear the Rabbit say to itself, "Oh dear! Oh dear! I shall be too late!" But when the Rabbit actually took a watch out of its waistcoat-pocket and looked at it and then hurried on, Alice started to her feet, for it flashed across her mind that she had never before seen a rabbit with either a waistcoat-pocket, or a watch to take out of it, and, burning with curiosity, she ran across the field after it and was just in time to see it pop down a large rabbit-hole, under the hedge. In another moment, down went Alice after it!

The rabbit-hole went straight on like a tunnel for some way and then dipped suddenly down, so suddenly that Alice had not a moment to think about stopping herself before she found herself falling down what seemed to be a very deep well.

Either the well was very deep, or she fell very slowly, for she had plenty of time, as she went down, to look about her. First, she tried to make out what she was coming to, but it was too dark to see anything; then she looked at the sides of the well and noticed that they were filled with cupboards and book-shelves; here and there she saw maps and pictures hung upon pegs. She took down a jar from one of the shelves as she passed. It was labelled 'ORANGE MARMALADE', but, to her great disappointment, it was empty; she did not like to drop the jar, so managed to put it into one of the cupboards as she fell past it.

Down, down, down! Would the fall never come to an end? There was nothing else to do, so Alice soon began talking to herself. "Dinah'll miss me very much to-night, I should think!" (Dinah was the cat.) "I hope they'll remember her saucer of milk at tea-time. Dinah, my dear, I wish you were down here with me!" Alice felt that she was dozing off, when suddenly, thump! thump! down she came upon a heap of sticks and dry leaves, and the fall was over.

Alice was not a bit hurt, and she jumped up in a moment. She looked up, but it was all dark overhead; before her was another long passage and the White Rabbit was still in sight, hurrying down it. There was not a moment to be lost. Away went Alice like the wind and was just in time to hear it say, as it turned a corner, "Oh, my

5

10

15

20

25

30

35

40

45

ears and whiskers, how late it's getting!" She was close behind it when she turned
the corner, but the Rabbit was no longer to be seen.

She found herself in a long, low hall, which was lit up by a row of lamps hanging
from the roof. There were doors all round the hall, but they were all locked; and   50
when Alice had been all the way down one side and up the other, trying every door,
she walked sadly down the middle, wondering how she was ever to get out again.

Suddenly she came upon a little table, all made of solid glass. There was nothing
on it but a tiny golden key, and Alice's first idea was that this might belong to one
of the doors of the hall; but, alas! either the locks were too large, or the key was too   55
small, but, at any rate, it would not open any of them. However, on the second time
round, she came upon a low curtain she had not noticed before, and behind it was
a little door about fifteen inches high. She tried the little golden key in the lock, and
to her great delight, it fitted!

Alice opened the door and found that it led into a small passage, not much larger   60
than a rat-hole; she knelt down and looked along the passage into the loveliest
garden you ever saw. How she longed to get out of that dark hall and wander about
among those beds of bright flowers and those cool fountains, but she could not
even get her head through the doorway. "Oh," said Alice, "how I wish I could shut
up like a telescope! I think I could, if I only knew how to begin."   65

Alice went back to the table, half hoping she might find another key on it, or at
any rate, a book of rules for shutting people up like telescopes. This time she found
a little bottle on it ("which certainly was not here before," said Alice), and tied round
the neck of the bottle was a paper label, with the words 'DRINK ME' beautifully
printed on it in large letters.   70

"No, I'll look first," she said, "and see whether it's marked '*poison*' or not," for
she had never forgotten that, if you drink from a bottle marked 'poison', it is almost
certain to disagree with you, sooner or later. However, this bottle was *not* marked
'poison', so Alice ventured to taste it, and, finding it very nice (it had a sort of mixed
flavour of cherry-tart, custard, pineapple, roast turkey, toffee and hot buttered toast),   75
she very soon finished it off.

From *Alice's Adventures in Wonderland* by Lewis Carroll

1 Why didn't Alice want to read the book?

_____

2 Why did Alice follow the rabbit? Give TWO reasons.

_____

_____

3 Explain why Alice thought that the well was very deep.

_____

_____

3

4 What does the author tell us about the rabbit? Find SIX pieces of evidence to support your answer.

B 2

_____

_____

_____

_____

3

5 Does Alice like orange marmalade? Use evidence from the text to support your answer.

B 2

_____

_____

2

6 In the extract, the word 'get' has been written as 'getting' (line 13).

B 2

  a Which grammar rule must be applied to 'get' before adding the 'ing' suffix?

_____

_____

  b Find another word in the first paragraph that has followed this rule.

_____

2

7 How did Alice dispose of the marmalade jar?

B 2

_____

1

8 Why do you think that Alice was sad as she walked down the middle of the hallway?

B 2

_____

_____

3

9 Find TWO different **similes** in the text.

B 2

_____

_____

2

10 Why didn't Alice see the door when she first tried to use the key? Give TWO reasons.

B 2

_____

_____

2

11 Describe, in your own words, what Alice could see behind the little door.

B 2

_____

_____

_____

_____

4

12 Which TWO items was Alice hoping to find on the glass table?

B 2

_____

2

13 What do you think is meant by each of these words as they are used in the text?

B 2

a remarkable (line 16) _____

b disagree (line 73) _____

c ventured (line 74) _____

3

14 Explain, in your own words, why Alice did not drink from the bottle straight away.

B 2

_____

_____

2

15 This adventure takes place on a cold winter's day. Do you agree with this statement? Refer to the text in your answer.

B 2

_____

_____

_____

2

16 Tick the THREE statements that are false.

B 2

A Alice was an only child. ☐

B The bottle tasted of six different flavours. ☐

C Alice turned into a telescope. ☐

D Alice had a pet called Dinah. ☐

E The bottle had a sticker on it labelled 'DRINK ME'. ☐

F Alice didn't think it was strange to hear a talking rabbit. ☐

3

… Already the storm had continued six days; on the seventh its fury seemed still increasing; and the morning dawned upon us without a prospect of hope, for no one on board even knew where we were. My four boys clung to me in their fright, while my wife wiped the tears from her cheeks.

At this moment a cry of "Land, land!" was heard through the roaring of the waves, and instantly the vessel struck against a rock so violently as to drive every one from his place; a tremendous cracking succeeded, as if the ship was going to pieces.

I hurried on deck, and saw a terrible sight. The crew had crowded into the boats till there was no room for us, and even as I appeared they cut the ropes to move off. I cried to them frantically not to leave us, but in vain, for the roaring of the sea prevented my being heard.

As all hope from this direction was over, I examined the ship to see if she would hold together for a little while, and was reassured. She was wedged stern first between two rocks, and it did not seem likely that the waves would drive her off at present. Therefore, when I returned to the cabin, which happened, fortunately, to be in the high part, and out of reach of the water, I was able to speak cheerfully of our position.

Comforted by this, my wife prepared something to eat, and the four boys at least ate heartily, and then the three youngest went to bed, and, tired out, soon were sleeping soundly. Fritz, the eldest, sat up with us.

"I have been thinking," he said, "that if we had some bladders or cork-jackets for mother and the others, you and I, father, could perhaps swim to land."

I thought there was some sense in what he said, so, in case the ship should break up in the night, he and I looked about for some small empty barrels; these we tied two and two together, and fastened them under the arms of each child.

Fritz then lay down, and was soon asleep; but his mother and I kept watch throughout this awful night. In the morning, the sky was brighter, and the wind had fallen.

The boys sprang up in capital spirits, and Fritz advised that we should swim to land while the sea was calm. Ernest, the second boy, protested, not being able to swim himself, and suggested a raft.

I sent them all to look about the ship, and bring what things they could find that were likely to be useful, while I and my wife discussed the situation.

Presently they all rejoined me, bringing various treasures. Fritz had two guns, some powder and shot and bullets; Ernest produced a lot of carpenters' tools; while Jack, the third boy, came up laughing on the back of a huge dog, named Turk, and followed by another called Flora. The poor creatures had almost knocked him down in their eagerness when he had released them; and though at first I thought more of the food they would eat than of their usefulness, I agreed they might certainly assist us in hunting should we ever get on shore.

Little Francis had found some fishing-hooks, at which his brothers mocked, until I reminded them it was likely we might have to depend for our food on fishing for some time to come.

My wife had found on board a cow and an ass, two goats, six sheep and a sow, which she had fed. All this was good so far as it went.

But now once more occurred to us the difficulty of crossing the broad strip of water that separated us from some kind of land, which we could just see far off. Jack, who was generally ready with an idea, cried out that he had often careered about on a pond at home in a tub, and that, as there seemed plenty of large barrels here, we might each have one and try. 50

This was not quite so simple as it sounded, but after some thinking I set to work, and, with the help of the boys, sawed four of the great barrels in half. This was tiring work, and took a long time, and there was much else to do before we could venture to trust ourselves on the water in them. 55

To make them more secure, we found a long pliant plank, and placed the eight tubs upon it, leaving a piece at each end reaching beyond the tubs. This being bent upward, like the keel of a vessel, made the whole contrivance more like a boat. We next nailed all the tubs to the plank, and afterwards put two other planks, of the same length as the first, on each side of the tubs. When all this was finished, we 60 found we had produced a kind of narrow boat, divided into eight compartments. But then the difficulty was to move this great boat at all, for its weight was enormous. However, by putting rollers under it and using all our strength, we launched it into the sea. I had taken the precaution to attach a rope to it first, so it rode tethered; but, alas! in the first moment, we saw that it leaned far over to one side in a most 65 alarming fashion. It soon occurred to me that this was only because it was so buoyant it danced up too far above the water, and after throwing some heavy things into the tubs, we saw it sink a little, and then float quite level.

However, all this had taken the whole day, and we had worked so hard that we had only eaten a bit of bread and taken a drink of milk occasionally, so now we sat 70 down to a regular supper, and then went to bed, in high expectation of getting to the land next morning.

From *The Swiss Family Robinson* by J.D. Wyss

1 How long did the storm last?

_____

2 How many people remained on the ship after the crew had left?

_____

3 How did the **narrator** know that the ship was stable?

_____

4 Which phrase explains that:

   a everyone on the ship was thrown around during the accident?

_____

   b Jack was an imaginative child?

_____

5 Reread the first paragraph. How does the author show that this is an adventure story from the start? Support your answer with FIVE pieces of evidence from this paragraph.

_____

_____

_____

_____

_____

6 Explain, in your own words, why small, empty barrels were tied under the arms of each child.

_____

_____

7 Explain why the youngest boy's find was so useful.

_____

_____

8 What do you think each of these words means as it is used in the text?

a heartily (line 20) _____

b capital (line 30) _____

c assist (line 42) _____

d careered (line 49) _____

9 Which TWO methods did the family use to launch the boat?

_____

_____

10 What do you think is meant by the following phrases?

a '… without a prospect of hope … ' (line 2)

_____

b '… a long pliant plank …' (line 56)

_____

c '… wedged stern first …' (line 14)

_____

11 Tick the THREE statements that are true.

    A The second youngest boy was called Jack. ☐

    B The three dogs were useful for hunting. ☐

    C They hoped to reach land on the ninth day. ☐

    D They used eight barrels to make their boat. ☐

    E There were 13 animals on board. ☐

    F The crew heard the family call after them. ☐

12 What do you think a bladder or cork-jacket would be useful for?

_____

13 Explain, in your own words, why and how the family stabilised their handmade craft. Refer to the text in your answer.

_____

_____

14 Why was it a sensible precaution to tether the boat?

_____

_____

15 Find an example of each of the following parts of speech in this sentence.

'This was tiring work, and took a long time, and there was much else to do before we could venture to trust ourselves on the water in them.'

a a **pronoun** _____   **b** a **conjunction** _____

c a **preposition** _____   **d** a **verb** _____

3

B 2

3

B 2

1

B 2

2

B 2

2

B 2

4

138 Green Lane,
Coventry
15th November 1940

Dearest Agnes,

I hope this letter finds you well. I'm writing this so that you know we are all safe   5
and sound after the horrors of last night. I just pray we never have to go through
anything like it again. It was six o'clock and we'd only just sat down to tea when
the sirens sounded. I wouldn't have minded but I'd used my last tin of corned beef
to make hash and I don't know when we'll get another. I wanted to try to put a
tin or two away in the run-up to Christmas but I never have enough coupons left   10
at the end of the week. How do you raise a growing family on rations? Churchill
keeps promising us that the end is in sight. It doesn't feel like it from where we're
standing.

Anyway, as I was saying, the sirens were ringing out; at the sound of which
Tom pulled a face but he quickly went out to do his A.R. Patrol and the children   15
and I grabbed our plates and went down into the shelter. Old Ma Pardoe from next
door was already there. She's still got the horrible winter flu that's going round,
so she was feeling particularly disgruntled. Unfortunately, by the time we'd got
settled, our tea was cold so we weren't feeling that cheerful either.

It was so dark and cold; even with our blankets we were perished. It was a right   20
miserable night and I couldn't wait for it to be over but then, oh Agnes, you
should have heard it! There was a deafening explosion right above and I knew; I
just knew that our house had taken a hit. Mr Pardoe came into the shelter and
said he'd seen a German parachute landing and our Dotty began crying. At that
moment, the parachute mine hit and the explosion was the worst I'd ever heard. I   25
felt sick to the pit of my stomach and we all started praying for Tom and the other
men out there doing the air raid patrol. Ma Pardoe began crying for her dog – all I
could think was "Fiddle the stupid dog, what about my Tom?"

Anyway, at that, twelve people all bundled into the shelter as theirs had come
under fire (before they had managed to get into it, thank God). They couldn't all   30
fit into ours though, so Mr Anderson, from Beanfield Avenue, and his neighbour
waited outside. I was sick with worry for them. Well, Mrs Anderson said that there
were bodies everywhere and that craters as big as houses had opened up! Apparently,
one of the emergency jeeps took a hit and a house on Beanfield had gone but a roof
beam had shot across the yard and smashed the window of old Ma Pardoe's house. If   35
anyone had been in that bedroom they wouldn't have stood a chance.

Poor Betsy was so afraid at the sound of the bombers continually overhead, that
she wet herself and I hadn't the heart to shout at the poor mite. The raid went on
and on. We took over eleven hours of hits all night and when we eventually did
get out, the sky was red. We were staring into the jaws of hell. The top of our house   40
has gone and the downstairs is only just standing, but the main thing is that

we've all survived – this time! Tom's got glass wounds to his face and hands but
he's been patched up and is doing okay.
  I hope you and Philip are all right. I'll pop by next Thursday as I've finished
knitting the gloves for Trevor and he certainly needs them in this weather.   45

  Love to you all from all of us.
  Hilda xxxxx

P.S. I forgot to tell you that Alice has had her baby – a little girl called Joyce
Sylvia who weighed in at 7 pounds 6 ounces. Can you believe she gave birth as
the bombers were flying overhead! Both mother and baby are doing fine.   50

Original text by Michellejoy Hughes

1 When did the sirens begin?

_____

B 2
1

2 In which season was this letter written? Find SIX pieces of evidence from the text
   to support your answer.

_____

_____

_____

_____

_____

_____

B 2
4

3 'Churchill keeps promising us that the end is in sight.' (lines 11–12). Which
   historical event do you think this sentence is referring to? Support your answer
   with FOUR pieces of evidence from the text.

_____

_____

_____

_____

B 2
4

4 Explain the meaning of the phrase '… they wouldn't have stood a chance'
   (line 36).

_____

_____

B 2
1

5 Why do you think that Hilda was 'sick with worry' (line 32)?

B 2

_____

_____

2

6 Reread this phrase: 'craters as big as houses' (line 33).

B 2

   a What do you think caused these craters to appear?

_____

   b Which literary technique is this phrase an example of?

2

_____

7 Explain what may have made Hilda think, "Fiddle the stupid dog" (line 28)?

B 2

_____

_____

2

8 This text is an informal letter. Find SIX pieces of evidence that support this statement.

B 2

_____

_____

_____

_____

_____

_____

6

9 How does Hilda make this letter sound frightening? Find SIX pieces of evidence to support your answer.

B 2

_____

_____

_____

_____

_____

_____

6

10 Find an example of a **metaphor** in the text.

B 2

_____

1

11 Underline the word that is closest in meaning to each given word as it is used in the text.

B 2

    a perished (line 20):   dying   frozen   hungry   scared

    b sound (line 6):   well   noisy   loud   happy

2

12 Imagine that you were one of the people in the shelter. Describe what it was like sitting in there. Refer to FOUR pieces of evidence from the text in your answer.

B 2

_____

_____

_____

_____

_____

_____

_____

4

Paper 4

I. THE PEAK DISTRICT

The wide-spreading moors of the Pennine chain stretch southward into Derbyshire. The whole of the county north of Castleton is a mountainous tract, called the Peak District; it consists for the most part of high and barren moorland, where sheep find scanty pasturage. Here and there high peaks rise above the rest, as the wild and rugged Kinderscout, with its tors, pools, and crags, and Mam Tor, which is nearly as high; none of these peaks is quite 2000 feet in height, but the district is so broken, rocky, and wild that it is truly mountain country. *(5)*

Deep, narrow valleys cross the moors, river valleys, with noisy mountain torrents dashing through them; while thick wood grows down the sides of these glens to the water's edge, and high crags rise among the trees. *(10)*

All the curious sights of the Peak District are not to be seen above ground. There are large and lofty caverns – chambers opening into the very heart of the mountains; some of them penetrating, room after room, a distance of more than half a mile. To explore these caverns one must have guides and torches; and surprising it is to see, within, every fantastic shape hanging from the roof or rising from the floor; now a fringe, deep and broken, now a miniature forest in stone, and now strange shapes of bird or beast. *(15)*

Have we got into a palace of the gnomes, and do they spend their years in thus adorning their chambers? *(20)*

The same unwearying artist has hewn these caverns out of the solid rock, and beautified them to suit his fantastic taste; a workman whose name you would little suspect. Soft as rain is and hard as some rocks are, there is none so hard but the rain will in time make a way through its substance. The mountain limestone of which these mountains are made is full of cracks; the rain does not all flow off the sides of the hills; much of it sinks through these cracks, down and down, wearing away the lime as it goes, and carrying the atoms along in its course. Sometimes the water forms for itself quite a wide channel; indeed, in limestone districts it often happens that a broad stream, a river, flows in at the mouth of a cavern, makes its way underground, and does not appear again for miles, and all this time the water has been wearing away the stone and enlarging the caverns. *(25) (30)*

The water does not carry away quite all the lime it wears from the rocks. Every tiny drop that falls from the roof of a cavern carries its own grains of lime. Some grains it leaves on the roof; some grains drop upon the floor. This goes on for ever, night and day, until at last the lime on the roof has made a little shoot, like an icicle, and the lime on the floor another little shoot rising up to meet it. There are many drops falling, side by side, and, in the course of ages, there is formed a sort of fringe, which hangs from the roof, as icicles might, while similar forms rise from below. These limestone droppings grow very, very slowly – it has taken many hundreds of years to make the strange figures in the caverns. Those on the roof are called stalactites, and those on the floor, stalagmites; two long names which come from a word in the Greek language, meaning, 'to drop'. *(35) (40)*

The Peak Cavern and Bagshaw Grotto are the largest in the district.

This mountain limestone contains a treasure besides the building stone, which is so excellent that some of it was carried to London to build the handsome *(45)*

Parliament Houses; this treasure is veins of lead ore, which occur from the Peak, southward, as far as Wirksworth, a great lead-mining place.

The Odin Mine, the Speedwell Mine, and the Bradwell Mine are in the Peak.

II. THE DALES

DERBYSHIRE, like Yorkshire, is famous for its beautiful dales. But in Derbyshire the Peak sends its spurs south instead of east; these long spurs reach into the middle of the county and separate the river valleys. 50

The Derwent valley is thus enclosed between hills, and a very beautiful valley it is, containing Chatsworth Park, the Duke of Devonshire's place. Farther south is Matlock, among hills; Abraham Heights, which the visitors climb upon donkeys, and High Tor, a giant crag with a steep face, are the best known heights. Matlock is a fashionable place, crowded with visitors in the summer, who come to drink, and to bathe in, the warm waters of the spring. 55

When the underground recesses become too full of water to hold any more, the water is forced out in springs: and when the water is forced up in this way from a great depth, the springs are warm; for the deeper we get into the earth's crust, the warmer it becomes. The water of these springs has often an exceedingly unpleasant taste, for the underground stream which at last breaks out in a spring does not carry lime only with it, but iron, or sulphur, or magnesia, or soda, or whatever substance it passes through. The waters of Matlock are good for consumptive and rheumatic patients. 60 65

There are two other watering-places with mineral springs in the lovely Wye valley, Bakewell and Buxton.

The most delightful of the dales of Derbyshire is Dovedale. The Dove is a tributary of the Trent which flows from Dove Head, near Buxton, where it rises, until it joins the Trent, between the two counties of Stafford and Derby. Here, the cliffs overhang the river, making dark, deep-looking pools; there, they open out; the woods come down to the river's brink, great crags jut out, and the blue stream gurgles over boulders at the bottom: now it is a wide river, and now so narrow and shallow, that it is crossed upon stepping-stones. 70 75

From *The Counties of England* by Charlotte Mason

1 Which part of Derbyshire is called the Peak District?

B 2

1

_____

2 What is Kinderscout (line 6)?

B 2

1

_____

3 Does the Peak District offer rich grazing land for animals? Explain your answer with reference to the text.

B 2

_____

_____

2

_____

4 Explain why the Peak District is referred to as 'mountain country' (line 8).

_____

_____

5 Give an alternative word that could replace each of these words as they are used in the text.

   a spurs (line 51) _____   **b** recesses (line 59) _____

   c brink (line 73) _____   **d** gurgles (line 73) _____

6 Who or what do you think the writer is referring to in each of these phrases?

   a '… noisy mountain torrents …' (line 9) _____

   b '… the same unwearying artist …' (line 21) _____

7 How are the caverns created? Refer to the text in your answer.

_____

_____

_____

_____

_____

8 Tick the TWO statements that are true.

   A Not all underground caverns are the same size. ☐

   B Limestone can be worn away and fractured. ☐

   C Rheumatic patients can benefit from a visit to Dovedale. ☐

   D The Duke of Derbyshire lives at Chatsworth Park. ☐

   E Coal is extracted from the ground at Speedwell Mine. ☐

9 Explain, in your own words, how both types of shoots are formed.

_____

_____

_____

_____

_____

10 Find an example of each of these parts of speech in this sentence.

'This goes on for ever, night and day, until at last the lime on the roof has made a little shoot, like an icicle, and the lime on the floor another little shoot rising up to meet it.'

a an **adjective** _____   b a **preposition** _____

c a **conjunction** _____   d a **pronoun** _____

B 2
4

11 In addition to the limestone, what can be found in the southward Peak?

_____

B 2
1

12 Why is Matlock popular with tourists?

_____

_____

B 2
2

13 Explain why some spring water might have a revolting taste.

_____

_____

B 2
1

14 Find a word in the text that means the same as cliffs or rockfaces.

_____

B 2
1

15 Explain, in your own words, how springs are created. Refer to the text in your answer.

_____

_____

_____

B 2
2

16 What is the Trent?

_____

B 2
1

17 Why do you think that the extract is divided into two sections?

_____

_____

B 2
1

Now go to the Progress Chart to record your score!   Total   35

Extract A

Mad Monkey Mayhem!

by Richard Preston

At the Swedish Furuvik Zoo, a 31-year-old male chimpanzee has provided scientific researchers with a vital insight into chimp behaviour. Recently, zookeepers have found that Santino, the chimp in question, has been throwing stones at visitors. This act isn't groundbreaking in itself but Santino appears to be different to other chimpanzees in that he carefully collects stones and then stores them in a hidden stockpile ready to use later. It is this 'forward planning' that has been hailed revolutionary by scientists.

Not only this, but Santino has also realised how to check which of the structural elements in his enclosure can be dismantled in order to create other missiles. Head ecologist Dr Torsten Hagstedt has regularly watched Santino knock gently against concrete blocks, looking for the weakest areas, and then apply more force to detach the loose pieces. Even more impressive has been the way in which he has shaped some of these concrete chunks into more aerodynamic weapons! These

Santino planning his next strike!

chunks have then been added to his growing stash of ammunition.

All of this extraordinary behaviour shows that Santino is able to plan ahead for when he is in a more aggressive state of mind. His ability to anticipate a future mood – that of aggression – is recognised by the chimp at times when he is actually feeling quite calm and relaxed. An interesting observation made by Dr Hagstedt is that Santino does not display any aggressive tendencies towards other chimps in his troop; rather, his distinct emotional outbursts are targeted purely towards human onlookers.

One of the psychologists who has been studying Santino's behaviour commented, "Santino ceases his activities when he notices a scientist or a keeper watching him, suggesting that he understands what it is to be 'sneaky' – like a naughty schoolboy! Not only can he consciously prepare for his future behaviour, but he also knows that what he is doing is 'bad'."

This complex pattern of 'forward planning' supports the belief that, to a certain degree, apes can plan their lives. In a captive environment it is not really necessary to plan ahead but, in the wild, this ability may be the most valuable skill an ape can have. Predicting events and preparing ahead of time for them, could, for example, help a chimpanzee to deal with a scarcity of food and the need to become an effective hunter. If an ape knows where dangers are, and can plan routes that avoid these dangers, it may aid its own survival and that of its young.

Researchers are now interested in widening their study further, in order to determine if this characteristic is displayed in other species. Santino was born in Germany at the Munich Zoo. He arrived in Sweden when he was five and continues to be one of the main attractions at the zoo.

Extract B

Chimpanzees are highly sociable creatures, living in extended family communities in rainforests, woodlands and grasslands. They can walk upright on two feet or on all fours but they also frequently swing from one tree to the next, enabling them to cover huge distances relatively quickly. They spend much of their time in the trees and also sleep in tree-top nests.   5

Chimpanzees are very resourceful. They use stones to break open nuts, leaves to soak up water (which they then drink from) and all manner of tools to shape nests, dig up insects and poke into logs to root out food.

Chimpanzees share 98% of our genetics. They are our closest living relatives, sharing a common ancestor who lived 4–8 million years ago. In scientific studies, some   10 apes have been taught basic sign language that they have first used to communicate with humans before going on to teach this form of language to their young.

Chimpanzee Facts and Figures

Type:	Mammal
Diet:	Omnivore – fruit, plants, insects, meat, eggs
Life span:	50 years in the wild, 60 years in captivity
Height:	1.2–1.7 m (4 ft–5 ft 5 in)
Weight:	32–60 kg (70–130 lbs)
Protection status:	Endangered species for their meat and the destruction of their natural habitat

Extract C

The antelope was scared for her baby. Nudging him carefully towards the rough tufts of grass, she encouraged him to eat quickly, carefully. "Build your strength, my lovely son. Build your strength and you will outrun your enemies and live a long life." The baby antelope ate and ate, but always with one eye on his mother.

The chimpanzee was scared for his baby. If the baby had no food, she would   5 die. The forests were diminishing, the hunters were always prowling with their guns. It was now or never. He called upon his brothers and together they went hunting. Soon, they spotted the antelopes grazing. At this, they lifted wooden sticks high above their heads.

The antelope saw a blaze of fur as she pushed her baby to the side. "Run my   10 boy, my lovely son." The mother ran to the left and to the right as the chimpanzees squealed and shrieked and shook their sticks and the baby antelope did run. He ran as swift as an eagle, fuelled by panic and fear. At last, he turned to look for his mother.

Exhausted, she ran left, right, left, and right again. She was fast, but she was no   15 match for a troop of chimpanzees. They circled her easily and she soon fell prey to their ravenous state.

On this hot, African night the chimpanzee fed his little baby. "Build your strength, my lovely daughter. Build your strength and you will outrun your enemies and live a long life." The baby chimpanzee ate and ate, but always with one eye on her father.   20

Original texts by Michellejoy Hughes

These questions are based on Extract A.

1 Which TWO countries are mentioned in the extract?

_____ and _____

2 Tick the ONE statement that is false.

A At times, Santino can appear relaxed. ☐

B Scientists believe that apes have the ability to anticipate events. ☐

C Santino has been at the zoo for more than 25 years. ☐

D Compared to other chimps, Santino seems to show a unique characteristic. ☐

E Santino likes people to stop and gaze at him in his enclosure. ☐

3 Find an example of a **collective noun** in the text. _____

4 Explain, in your own words, why Santino shaped some of the loosened concrete pieces.

_____

_____

5 The term 'groundbreaking' has been used in line 7. Find another word in the text that has a similar meaning.

_____

6 Explain, in your own words, how the skill that Santino has shown could be useful to an ape in the wild.

_____

_____

_____

7 What type of source do you think this extract has been taken from? Support your answer with FOUR pieces of evidence.

_____

_____

_____

_____

These questions are based on Extract B.

8 What do you think an omnivore is?

_____

9 Find TWO reasons why chimpanzees could become extinct.

_____

_____

10 Give an alternative word for each of these words as they are used in the extract.

   a frequently (line 3) _____

   b resourceful (line 6) _____

   c enabling (line 3) _____

11 Chimpanzees are solitary creatures. Do you agree with this statement? Support your answer with reference to the text.

_____

_____

_____

These questions are based on Extract C.

12 Which THREE wishes did both parents have for their young?

_____

_____

_____

13 Why did the chimpanzees attack the antelopes?

_____

14 Why do you think that the adult antelope was captured so easily?

_____

_____

15 Find an example of each literary technique in the text.

   a alliteration _____

   b a **simile** _____

21

This question is based on more than one extract.

16 Chimpanzees are intelligent animals. Do you agree with this statement? Support your answer with FIVE pieces of evidence. You should refer to more than one text in your answer.

_____

_____

_____

_____

_____

_____

_____

5

Now go to the Progress Chart to record your score!   Total   35

Answers will vary for questions that require children to answer in their own words. Possible answers to these questions are either given in italics or written as bulleted lists.

Paper 1

1 The book didn't contain any pictures or conversations (lines 5–6).

2 [1] mark for any two of these points:
 • She was bored / had nothing to do (line 3).
 • She had never seen a rabbit either wearing a waistcoat or a pocket-watch (lines 22–23).
 • She was 'burning with curiosity' to find out more (line 23).

3 She had a lot of time to look around her as she was falling (line 29).

4 [½] mark for each of these points:
 The reader is told that the rabbit:
 • is white (line 14)
 • has pink eyes (line 15)
 • is able to talk (line 19)
 • wears clothes (line 20)
 • can tell the time (line 20)
 • is in a hurry / is late for an appointment (line 19).

5 *Yes, Alice does like orange marmalade* [1] *because she was disappointed to find that the jar was empty* [1] (line 35).

6 a *If a word ends with a single consonant that is preceded by a short vowel sound, double the consonant and then add 'ing'.*
 b 'beginning' (line 1) or 'sitting' (line 2)

7 She placed it into a cupboard as she was falling down past it.

8 [1] mark for each point:
 • The White Rabbit had disappeared / Alice was alone (line 48).
 • All of the doors she tried were locked (line 50).
 • She did not know if she would be able to get out (line 52).

9 [1] mark each for any two of these similes:
 • 'The rabbit hole went straight on like a tunnel …' (line 26)
 • 'Away went Alice like the wind …' (lines 45–46)
 • '… I wish I could shut up like a telescope!' (lines 64–65)
 • '… a book of rules for shutting people up like telescopes' (line 67).

10 [1] mark for each point:
 • The door was hidden behind a low curtain that she hadn't noticed before (line 57).
 • The door was very small, only about fifteen inches high (line 58).

11 *Alice could see a small passageway that was about the same size as a rat-hole* [1] (lines 60–61). *At the end of this, there was a beautiful garden* [1] (lines 61–62), *containing bright flower beds* [1] (line 63) *and cool-looking fountains* [1] (line 63).

12 [1] mark for each point:
 • a key (line 66)
 • a book that would show her how to shut up like a telescope (line 67)

13 a *unusual*
 b *upset*
 c *dared, decided*

14 *Alice first wanted to check that the bottle was safe to drink from* [1] *because she knew that if it was marked 'poison' it would make her ill* [1]. (lines 71–73)

15 *No, it cannot be winter because:* [1] mark each for any two of these points:
 • It was warm enough for Alice and her sister to be sitting on the bank (line 2).
 • Alice considered picking some daisies to make a daisy chain – daisies are not out in winter (lines 9–14).
 • The garden behind the little door has beds of bright flowers and flowing fountains – this suggests it is either spring or summer (line 63).

16 A (line 2), C (lines 64–65), E (line 69)

Paper 2

1 Seven days (line 1; lines 28–29)

2 Six people

3 The ship was jammed firmly between two rocks so it was unlikely that the sea would dislodge her (lines 14–15).

4 a '… as to drive every one from his place …' (lines 6–7)
 b 'Jack, who was generally ready with an idea…' (line 49)

5 [1] mark for each point:
 • The reader joins the story during a violent storm (line 1).
 • The force of the storm was increasing (line 1).
 • The characters were faced with little hope (line 2).

- They were lost (lines 2–3).
- The narrator's four sons were scared and his wife was crying (lines 3–4).

6 *Barrels are buoyant and would be good floating aids* [1], *so they tied them under the arms of each child in case the ship broke into pieces during the night* [1] (line 26).

7 *Francis found some fishing-hooks,* [1] *which would be useful if the family were to rely on fish as a main source of food for some time* [1] (lines 44–46).

8 a *cheerfully, enthusiastically*
  b *excellent*
  c *help*
  d *hurtled, raced*

9 [1] mark for each point:
  - They placed rollers underneath the boat (line 63).
  - They used their body weight / strength to push it into the sea (line 63).

10 a it was a hopeless situation / there was no chance of rescue
  b a long, flexible piece of wood
  c the back of the ship was trapped

11 A (line 37), C (lines 71–72), E (lines 37–38 and 45)

12 *Bladders or cork-jackets are types of buoyancy aid that would help someone or something to float.*

13 *The craft was too light,* [1] (lines 66–67) *so they threw some heavy objects into it to make it float level* [1] (lines 67–68).

14 [1] mark for each of these (or similar) points:
  Tethering their craft would:
  - *stop it from floating away*
  - *allow them to control it*

15 a This / we / ourselves / them
  b and / before
  c in / on
  d was tiring / took / was / to do / could venture / to trust

Paper 3

1 six o'clock / 6pm

2 *This letter was written in winter* [1] *because:*
  [½] mark for each of these points:
  - the date is given as 15th November (line 3)
  - it is nearly Christmas (line 10)
  - Old Ma Pardoe has winter flu (line 17)
  - it is already dark outside at 6pm (line 20)

- the weather is cold (line 20)
- Trevor needs gloves (line 45).

3 [1] mark each for any four of these points:
  This sentence is referring to the Second World War because the letter mentions:
  - air raid sirens (line 8)
  - food coupons (line 10)
  - food rations (line 11)
  - the A.R Patrol (line 15)
  - air raid shelters (line 16)
  - explosions overhead and a house being 'hit' (lines 22–23)
  - a German parachute landing (line 24)
  - a parachute mine (line 25)
  - bodies lying around (line 33)
  - craters in the ground (line 33)
  - bombers flying overhead (line 37)
  Also, the letter:
  - is dated November 1940 (line 3)
  - implies that Churchill is the Prime Minister (lines 11–12).

4 They would have been killed straight away.

5 *Hilda felt sick with worry for the men because they were outside in the cold* [1] *and without the protection of the shelter they were more likely to be injured or killed* [1].

6 a The bombs dropped by the bombers overhead.
  b a simile

7 [1] mark each for any two of these (or similar) points:
  - Hilda thought that Ma Pardoe should be more concerned about people instead of her dog.
  - Hilda was more worried about her husband Tom than an animal.
  - Hilda thought Ma Pardoe was selfish thinking only of herself.

8 [1] mark each for any six of these points:
  - The text has been handwritten.
  - The sender's address has been written in the top right-hand corner (lines 1–2).
  - The date has been written under the address (line 3).
  - The text begins with a standard opening (line 4).
  - The text is written in a chatty, informal style / contains a personal account.
  - The text has been written in the first person.
  - The text has been signed by the writer (line 47).

- The standard closing includes 'kisses' (line 47).
- A P.S. has been added at the end (lines 48–50).

9 [1] mark each for any six of these points:
Hilda makes this letter sound frightening by:
- referring to 'the horrors of last night' (line 6)
- stating that she never wishes to experience the same events again (lines 6–7)
- implying the urgency with which she and the children had to go to the shelter (lines 15–16)
- stating that it was dark and cold outside (line 20)
- referring to the first explosion as 'deafening' and being 'right above' them (line 22)
- referring to the second explosion as being nothing like she had ever heard (line 25)
- referring to her sense of fear (line 26)
- stating that everyone in the shelter was 'praying' (line 26)
- stating that the shelter wasn't large enough to hold everyone inside (lines 30–31)
- including the image of dead bodies lying everywhere (line 33)
- stating that Betsy was so scared she wet herself (lines 37–38)
- describing the sky as 'red' and the scene of devastation as 'hell' (line 40)
- implying that they might not all be so lucky next time (line 42)
- stating that Tom was wounded in the face (line 42).

10 '... staring into the jaws of hell' (line 40)
11 a frozen
   b well
12 [1] mark each for reference to any four of these (or similar) points:
- The darkness (line 20)
- The perishing cold (line 20)
- The scary, deafening noises overhead (line 22)
- The sound of Dotty crying (line 24)
- The worry for family and friends who may be outside the shelter (line 32)
- Feeling crushed in the overcrowded space (line 29)
- The fear at being told of the devastation outside (lines 32–36)
- The sense of relief at coming out after being bombarded for 11 hours (line 42).

1 The whole of the county north of Castleton. (line 3)
2 a mountain
3 [1] mark for each point:
No, the land is not good for grazing because:
- it is a high and barren moorland (line 4)
- sheep find it difficult to find good pastures (lines 4–5).

4 [1] mark each for any two of these points:
- The whole area is a 'mountainous tract' (line 3)
- There are many high peaks (line 5)
- Kinderscout is described as 'wild and rugged' (lines 5–6)
- Some mountains have tors and crags (line 6)
- The land is described as 'broken, rocky and wild' (lines 7–8).

5 a *branches*, *shoots*
   b *nooks*, *spaces*
   c *edge*
   d *ripples*, *babbles*
6 a the river
   b the rain
7 *Limestone is full of cracks* [1] (lines 24–25). *Rain seeps deep down into the earth through these cracks* [1] (line 26). *As the water travels through the limestone, the stone is gradually eroded away making caverns* [1] (lines 30–31). *The continual erosion of the stone makes these caverns larger* [1] (line 31).
8 A (line 13), B (lines 26–27)
9 *The water that flows through the rocks doesn't wash away all of the lime* [1] (line 32). *Some grains of lime are left on the roof of the cavern, while other lime particles drip on to the floor* [1] (lines 33–34). *This continual process eventually causes icicle shapes to form, dangling from the roof (stalactites) and building up from the floor (stalagmites)* [1] (lines 35–36). *This process happens extremely slowly, over many years* [1] (lines 39–40).
10 a little
   b on / up
   c until / and
   d this / it
11 lead ore (lines 46–47)
12 [1] mark each for any two of these points:
- Matlock is a fashionable place to visit (line 57).

- The water is extremely good to drink (line 57).
- People want to bathe in the warm spring waters (line 58).

13 *Spring water can contain a range of minerals other than lime, such as iron, sulphur, magnesium* (magnesia)*, and soda which give it an unpleasant taste* (lines 62–65).

14 crags (line 6)

15 *A spring appears when a deep underground pool can no longer hold the amount of rain water that has collected in it* [1] (lines 59–60). *At this point, the water is forced upwards out of the ground* [1] (line 60).

16 a river

17 [1] mark for either of these two points:
- Breaking the text into two sections makes it easier for the reader to follow.
- Each section discusses a separate part of the county.

Paper 5

1 Germany, Sweden

2 E (lines 38–40)

3 troop (line 38)

4 *Santino shaped some of the loosened pieces into sleeker, smoother missiles,* [1] *so that they would be able to travel further and faster when thrown.* [1]

5 revolutionary (line 13)

6 *Being able to predict events and plan ahead would be a useful skill to have in the wild because it could help a chimpanzee to prepare for times when food is scarce* [1] (lines 57–59), *to develop successful hunting skills* [1] (lines 57–58) *and to avoid any known dangers, aiding survival* [1] (lines 62–63).

7 *This text is likely to have been taken from a magazine article* [1] *because the text:* [1] mark each for any four of these points:
- includes a 'weekly features' running title across the top
- has a slogan heading
- has a byline
- includes a picture with a caption
- is written in a factual, formal, unbiased style
- finishes with a lead to next week's feature article.

8 Someone or something that eats any kind of food.

9 [1] mark for each point:
- People hunt chimpanzees to eat (line 19).

- Their natural environment is being destroyed, leaving fewer places for them to live (lines 19–20).

10 a *regularly, often*
   b *inventive, imaginative*
   c *allowing, permitting*

11 *The text suggests that chimpanzees are not solitary creatures* [1] *because it states that they are highly sociable and live in extended family communities* [1] (line 1).

12 [1] mark for each point:
- Develop strength (line 2, 3; line 18)
- Ability to outrun enemies (line 3; line 19)
- Live a long life (lines 3–4; lines 19–20)

13 [1] mark for either of these points:
- The chimpanzee knew that his baby would die if he did not find food (lines 5–6).
- All of the chimpanzees were hungry (line 7).

14 [1] mark each for any two of these points:
- The chimpanzees had sticks to use as weapons (line 8).
- The antelope was extremely tired (line 15).
- It was difficult for one antelope to outrun a group of chimpanzees (lines 15–16).

15 a [1] mark for any one of these examples:
- '… live a long life' (lines 3–4; lines 19–20)
- '… antelope ate and ate …' (line 4)
- '… squealed and shrieked and shook their sticks …' (line 12)

   b 'He ran as swift as an eagle …' (lines 12–13)

16 [1] mark each for any five of these points:
Yes, chimpanzees are intelligent because there is evidence that they:
- can forward plan (Extract A, line 12)
- can recognise that they experience different moods (Extract A, lines 31–32)
- can recognise 'right' from 'wrong' (Extract A, lines 48–49)
- can easily adapt their method of movement – 2 legs, 4 legs, swinging (Extract B, lines 2–3)
- share 98% of human genes (Extract B, line 9)
- can learn to communicate with humans (Extract B, lines 11–12)
- can work together as a pack to hunt (Extract C, line 7)
- can analyse objects and consider how they can be used – they are resourceful (Extract A, lines 14–17; Extract B, lines 6–8)
- can build and use weapons (Extract A, lines 23–25; Extract C, line 8).

Paper 6

1 the train

2 *The poem suggests that the train was moving quickly* [1] *because*: [½] mark for each point:
- it was travelling faster than fairies (line 1)
- it was travelling faster than witches (line 1)
- it was 'charging' forward (line 3)
- the sights of the countryside were 'flying' past (lines 5–6)
- stations disappeared in the wink of an eye (lines 7–8)
- only a quick glimpse of each sight could be caught (line 16).

3 [1] mark for each simile:
- '… charging along like troops in a battle…' (line 3)
- '… Fly as thick as driving rain; …' (line 6)

4 the train

5 [1] mark each for any five of these points:
The text:
- is presented in two verses
- is written in rhyming couplets / the last word of each line rhymes with the last word of the line above / below it
- has a clear rhythm when read
- is made up of short lines
- begins each new line with a capital letter
- uses sound effects such as alliteration (line 1)
- uses punctuation to create rhythmic effects
- includes imagery, e.g. similes.

6 *No, the train doesn't stop* [1] *because the poem states that* 'painted stations whistle by' [1] (line 8).

7 a travelling in a bumpy manner
  b the different sights disappear out of view very quickly

8 *This poem has been written for children / young readers* [1] *because it*: [1] mark for each of these four (or similar) points:
- refers to fairies and witches (line 1)
- does not use overly complex words
- is quite short, consisting of only two verses
- uses pairs of rhyming phrases.

9 a threw
  b sites
  c reign / rein

10 [1] mark each for any three of these (or similar) points:
- Everything is seen through the window, as the train passes through it.
- The writer refers to the passing meadows, hill, plain – these are static objects so he must be moving.
- The writer uses the phrase 'here is' several times, showing that he has reached a new sight.
- The writer must be moving forward quickly, as he states that he only gets a quick glimpse of each sight before it is gone forever – he cannot go back to look at it.

11 [1] mark each for any three of these points:
The writer makes the words sound like a train journey by:
- using rhyming words to create patterns that echo a train's movement
- making patterns and rhythms with the syllables of words
- alternating between long and short words to create a rhythm
- using punctuation to control the speed of the poem.

12 a troughs
   b hurtling
   c climbs

13 D

Paper 7

1 [1] mark for each point:
- She was cold (line 11)
- She was scared (line 11)

2 *The children hid behind a log that was lying on the ground* [1] (lines 14–15) *and they completely covered themselves in snow* [1] (lines 16–19).

3 a the snow was packed firmly to give them protection
  b the snow melted into a pool of water that kept growing larger

4 'rampaging pirates' (line 38)

5 a 'They stood like statues …'
  b '… pillaged and plundered …'

6 [1] mark each for any three of these points:
- The snow was deep, which made it difficult to move in (line 1).
- The trees blocked many of the paths (lines 1–2).
- Fallen logs lay hidden under the snow, making moving quickly difficult (line 2).
- They had to be quiet (line 9).
- They had to stop and check if they were being followed (lines 4–5).

- The village was a long way away, on the other side of the forest (lines 45–46).
- It was geting dark (line 59).

7 *To calm herself and help her focus, Afeefa prayed* [1] *(line 27) and repeated the same meditative words over and over in her head* [1] *(lines 27–29).*

8 [1] mark for each point:
- Haajid knew that they would be discovered if he screamed (line 31–32).
- If they were discovered, they would be killed or imprisoned like the other villagers (line 32).
- If they were killed or imprisoned then there would be no one left to try to find help and the rest of the village would be doomed (lines 31–35).

9 a daylight / tinge / snow
b waning / casting
c yellow / sickly
d across

10 [1] mark each for any four of these points:
- Homes were taken (line 37).
- Possessions were snatched (line 37).
- Villagers were imprisoned or killed (line 36).
- The villagers' lives were made worthless (line 37).
- The quiet peaceful neighbourhood became a graveyard (line 39–40).

11 a *heard*
b *fading*

12 *The man means that his colleague should have killed all of the children in the first place, as he was meant to have done.*

13 [1] mark each for any three of these points:
Being buried in snow:
- is a painful experience (line 20)
- makes you very wet (line 20)
- chills you to the bone and makes you numb (lines 20–21)
- makes your skin sting (line 21)
- makes you wet and causes you to shiver (line 23).

14 *A new snow fall would cover their footprints* [1] *(line 62) and make it harder for the men to follow them on their new route* [1]

15 [1] mark for each point:
- They wanted to finish off the job that was started in the village (line 52).
- They wanted to confirm that the children were dead (line 54).

Paper 8

1 He was not born with any particularly special skills or ability (lines 11–12).

2 [1] mark each for any three of these points:
- He was teased for being bottom of the class (lines 34–35).
- He was called stupid by the boy who was top of the class (line 34).
- The boy told his classmates that he was useless (line 35).
- He fought the boy and won but felt guilty for using violence (lines 40–42).
- He decided to beat the boy through academic success, not through fighting (lines 42–43).

3 *Newton did not succeed as a farmer* [1] *because the text states that he regularly forgot where he was meant to be and what he was supposed to be doing* [1] *(line 56) and that he preferred reading to farming* [1] *(lines 56–57).*

4 'I like to think with my brain and then create with my fingers.' (lines 68–69).

5 1664

6 B (lines 23–24), C (line 53)

7 a I had reached breaking point and could not continue any further
b to continue the work of my father and do the job that he had done
c to walk around reading a book and not paying attention to what else was around

8 a *basic*
b *academics, intellectuals*
c *practising, following*
d *persevered, continued*

9 *Newton first jumped in the same direction as the wind was blowing* [1] *(line 72) and then he recorded how far he had jumped* [1] *(lines 72–73). He could then compare how strong the wind was by how far it had helped him to jump* [1] *(line 73).*

10 *Newton decided to do something meaningful with his life after the Great Plague* [1] *(line 82), during which many of the boys he knew who lived in London died* [1] *(lines 80–81).*

11 Gravity is the natural force that keeps us on the ground (line 93).

12 [1] mark each for any four of these points:
Newton:
- shuffles as he walks (line 4)
- wears thick-rimmed glasses (line 9)

- has thick, grey hair (line 83)
- is wearing a suit jacket that is too small for him (line 105)
- has not tucked his shirt into his trousers (line 106).

13 *This extract has been taken from a playscript* [1] *because*: [1] mark each for any six of these points:
- the heading is given as Act I, Scene 1
- the name of (or abbreviation for) each character is written at the start of each piece of dialogue
- a colon is used to separate a character's name from their speech
- the text consists mainly of dialogue
- no speech marks are used in the dialogue
- a new line is started each time a different character speaks
- stage directions are written in italics.

Paper 9

1 21 miles
2 [1] mark for each point:
- The Channel has dangerous currents (line 4).
- Fierce winds sweep over this stretch of water (line 4).
3 [1] mark for each point:
- The land between England and France sank below sea level (lines 11–12).
- The land between Scotland and Norway sank below sea level (line 12).
- The sea covered the low ground to form Ireland and the smaller islands (line 14).
4 *The sea and land battled for many years* [1] *over which parts of the land would stay above sea level and which sections would be claimed by the sea.* [1]
5 [1] mark for each point:
The sea:
- protected the British Isles from invasion (lines 18–19)
- provided people with plenty of fish to eat (line 20)
- gave people a trading route with other countries (lines 21–22)
- ensured that it rained regularly, helping the growth of crops (lines 19–20).
6 a coal (line 36)
  b Teutons (line 65)
  c Celts (line 63)
  d bronze (line 77)

7 'mountainous' (line 38)
8 Western Asia [1] (line 60), Eastern Europe [1] (line 60)
9 [1] mark each for any six of these points:
The Briton:
- is tall (line 72)
- is slender (line 72)
- has a fair complexion (line 72)
- has blue eyes (line 72)
- has red hair (line 73)
- has a stained blue face and body (lines 73–74)
- is on foot (line 74)
- is carrying a sword and a spear (line 75).
10 D (line 39), E (line 84)
11 [1] mark for each point:
The Druids were:
- priests (line 90)
- educated or learned men (line 91)
- well-respected (line 91)
- consulted on questions of law and religion (line 92).
12 Stonehenge is likely to be a religious structure that was built as a place of worship (lines 98–99).
13 [1] mark for each point:
- The Britons were not ruled or governed by one leader (lines 102–103).
- The British Isles were not united so presented no combined resistance (line 104).
- The Romans had stricter discipline and firmer organisation than the Britons (line 105).

Paper 10

1 24th December
2 The children were dreaming of sugar-plums (lines 5–6).
3 the children's father
4 *The house was quiet before St Nick arrived* [1] *because the poem states that 'Not a creature was stirring, not even a mouse'* [1] (line 2).
5 [1] mark for each point:
- The moon was shining (lines 13–14).
- The snow was white and reflected the moon (lines 13–14).
6 a type of window
7 a 'His cheeks were like roses…' / '… his nose like a cherry!'
  b '… encircled his head like a wreath.' / 'like a bowful of jelly'
  c '… they all flew like the down of a thistle.'

8 a he was unsure of what he would see / he was surprised at what he saw

  b in a flash / quickly

9 'more rapid than eagles' (line 19)

10 Dancer

11 St Nick winked at him [1] (line 47) *and nodded / twisted his head towards him* [1] (lines 50–52).

12 [½] mark for each point:

St Nick:
- was little (line 17)
- was old (line 17, 45)
- was sprightly (lively and quick) (line 17)
- was dressed in a fur suit (line 33)
- was covered in ash and soot (line 34)
- was carrying a sack full of toys that made him look like a peddler / toy seller (line 36)
- had sparkling eyes (line 37)
- had dimples (line 37)
- had rosy cheeks (line 38)
- had a red nose (line 38)
- had a funny little mouth (line 39)
- had a white beard (line 40)
- was smoking a pipe (line 41)
- had a broad / wide face (line 43)
- had a small, round belly (line 43)
- was chubby (line 45).

13 a *heads*

  b *stained*, *marked*

  c *pack*, *sack*

14 [1] mark each for any two of these homophone pairs:
- I – eye / aye
- knew – new
- in – inn
- be – bee

15 [1] mark each for any five of these points:

The reader is given the impression that St Nick is a happy person because the poems states that:
- his eyes twinkled (line 37)
- he had 'merry' dimples (line 37)
- he had rosy cheeks (line 38)
- he had a funny little mouth (line 39)
- his little round belly shook when he laughed (line 43–44)
- he was a 'jolly old elf' (line 45)
- he wished everyone a Happy Christmas (line 56).

Paper 6

Faster than fairies, faster than witches,
Bridges and houses, hedges and ditches;
And charging along like troops in a battle
All through the meadows the horses and cattle:
All of the sights of the hill and the plain   5
Fly as thick as driving rain;
And ever again, in the wink of an eye,
Painted stations whistle by.

Here is a child who clambers and scrambles,
All by himself and gathering brambles;   10
Here is a tramp who stands and gazes;
And here is the green for stringing the daisies!
Here is a cart run away in the road
Lumping along with man and load;
And here is a mill, and there is a river: 15
Each a glimpse and gone forever!

From a Railway Carriage by Robert Louis Stevenson

1 What was faster than a fairy?

_____

2 Do you think that the train was moving quickly or slowly? Support your answer
   with SIX pieces of evidence from the text.

_____

_____

_____

_____

_____

_____

3 Find TWO **similes** in the poem.

_____

_____

4 What or who was charging along?

_____

5 This text is an example of a poem. Find FIVE pieces of evidence from the text that support this statement.

_____

_____

_____

_____

_____

6 Does the train stop to pick up passengers? Explain your answer with reference to the text.

_____

_____

7 What do you think these phrases mean in the context of the poem?

a '… Lumping along …' (line 14)

_____

b '… Each a glimpse and gone forever' (line 16)

_____

8 Which type of reader do you think this poem has been written for? Support your answer with FOUR pieces of evidence from the poem.

_____

_____

_____

_____

9 Write a **homophone** for each of these words.

a through _____ **b** sights _____ **c** rain _____

10 How do you know that the writer is on the train? Refer to THREE pieces of evidence in your answer.

_____

_____

_____

11 How does the writer make the words of the poem *sound* like a train journey? Refer to the text to support your answer.

B 2

_____

_____

_____

_____

○ 3

12 Underline the ONE word that could replace each given word as it is used in the poem.

B 2

   a ditches (line 2):   troughs   throws   catches   passages   roads

   b charging (line 3):   accusing   costing   hurtling   walking   singing

   c clambers (line 9):   ducks   eats   snatches   hides   climbs

○ 3

13 Tick the ONE statement that is false.

B 2

   A There are animals in the meadows. ☐

   B The train passes a boy as it travels along. ☐

   C The train travels through the countryside. ☐

   D It rains during the journey. ☐

   E A cart is rolling quickly down a road. ☐

○ 1

Now go to the Progress Chart to record your score!   **Total** ○ 35

The heavy snow made it difficult for them to find their way. Trees blocked many routes whilst fallen logs lay in wait like sleeping giants who might, at a moment's notice, jump up with a shout. No bird sound could be heard. All was still other than the crisp crunch of fresh snow when they moved. They stood like statues, straining their ears to hear for any noise. Haajid grabbed his sister's arm suddenly and   5
pointed to the left. Afeefa could hear nothing but then, like a whisper on the gentlest of breezes, she heard a slow crunch of the snow. They looked at each other, united in their feelings of fear and not knowing what to do for the best. If they moved, they would be heard although they may already have given away their position. If they stood still, they may be found soon and then they would have no options left.   10

Afeefa could feel her knees shaking, partly due to the cold and partly due to fear. Haajid felt the responsibility of being the oldest and as he prayed for wisdom and courage they heard another crunch of the snow. Only this time it was much more distinctive. Haajid made a decision. Pushing his sister onto the ground behind a fallen log where they stood, he frantically began covering her body with snow. She   15
instinctively knew what he was doing and, as quietly as was possible, she covered her own hair and shoulders with the snow. Haajid crept over another fallen log and he too began to cover his clothing and hair, pushing the soft, feather-light snow until it compacted into a coat of armour.

Afeefa tried to block out her feelings of pain as the wet, frozen snow chilled her to   20
a bone-cold numbness. Stinging around her neck and face, she concentrated hard to stop her body from shivering. How long would she be able to bear the unbearable? Haajid had also begun to shiver from the wet sensation against his skin which trickled slowly, finding the lowest point of his back as it puddled and swelled.

Another crunch, and then another. The footsteps were definitely getting closer.   25
Afeefa could sense the vibrations as the footsteps passed the fallen log. She held her breath and prayed, reciting in her brain the words that helped her focus. Like patterns and rhythms they swallowed her fear and her pain, their meditative quality soothing her nerves and comforting her mind.

Haajid could see the shadow cast over the snow barely a metre away from his   30
body. He wanted to scream in anguish but knew that such a foolish action would set into place a chain reaction that would surely end in the death of all of them. He thought about his mother, sick with fright, praying that her two children would make it to safety. He thought about his father; unable to comfort his wife, as they would surely be imprisoned in separate areas.   35

How could a whole village be subjected to such cruelty? How could their homes be taken, their possessions snatched, their lives made worthless? And for what reason? Like rampaging pirates, the enemy had pillaged and plundered to their hearts' content. Overnight, the village had changed from a quiet, peaceful neighbourhood to a graveyard.   40

How many children had escaped with Afeefa and Haajid? He tried to count them in his head. Maybe thirteen, maybe fifteen but now how many were left? Just the two of them. Two people free out of a village of over three hundred. Would the adults still be alive? Haajid had no idea of time or where they were exactly. He just knew that he needed to cross the forest and then maybe, just maybe he would find   45
a place of refuge in the next village.

The footsteps had stopped. The shadow of the man had passed. Haajid wondered when it would be safe to move. Just as he was about to sit up he heard a man whisper to another.

"The kids aren't here. I don't think any of them survived. I took a hit at them all." 50

The second man responded, "You took a hit but you didn't kill them all, did you? If you'd done a proper job we wouldn't be here searching for them."

"Just relax; yes, they're not here are they?" replied the first man.

"I'll relax when I see the bodies in front of me. Until then we hunt them down."

The two men continued talking but they were now too far away for words to be 55 distinguished.

Haajid closed his eyes for a minute and tried to gather any strength that he had left. Getting out of the forest was not going to be easy but he knew it had to be attempted. The daylight was waning, casting a yellow, sickly tinge across the snow. Survival was critical. The time to move was now. Haajid sat up carefully and looked 60 around him. He could see the footprints laying a trail to the right. They would have to destroy their footprints or hope that new snow would fall. Helping his sister up, Haajid then set a course due north. It was their only hope …

Original text by Michellejoy Hughes

1 Find TWO reasons that explain why Afeefa felt unsteady. **B 2**

_____ **2**

_____

2 Explain, in your own words, the TWO ways in which the children concealed themselves. **B 2**

_____

_____

_____ **2**

3 What do you think is meant by each of the following phrases? **B 2**

   a '… compacted into a coat of armour' (line 19) _____

   b '… it puddled and swelled' (line 24) _____ **2**

4 Which two-word phrase describes the bandits? **B 2**

_____ **1**

5 Find ONE example of each literary technique in the given section of text. **B 2**

   a a **simile** (lines 3–5) _____

   b **alliteration** (lines 36–40) _____ **2**

6 Why do you think it was difficult for the children to reach the next village? Refer to the text in your answer.

_____

_____

_____

7 Explain how Afeefa calmed herself as she lay under the snow.

_____

_____

8 Why does Haajid think that screaming would cause a chain reaction?

_____

_____

_____

9 Find an example of each of the following parts of speech in this sentence.

'The daylight was waning, casting a yellow, sickly tinge across the snow.'

a **noun** _____   b **verb** _____

c **adjective** _____   d **preposition** _____

10 How did the village change? Find FOUR pieces of evidence to support your answer.

_____

_____

_____

_____

11 Give an alternative word that could replace each of these words as they are used in the text.

a **distinguished** (line 56) _____   b **waning** (line 59) _____

12 What does the man mean when he says, "If you'd done a proper job ..." (line 52)?

_____

_____

13 How might the children have described their experience of being covered with snow? Refer to THREE pieces of evidence in the text in your answer.

_____

_____

_____

_____

14 Why does Haajid hope for new snow to fall?

_____

_____

15 Why did the men want to find the two children? Refer to the text in your answer.

_____

_____

_____

_____

Now go to the Progress Chart to record your score!   Total   35

Act I, Scene 1

[Emily Beddall (EB) walks onto stage greeted by audience cheers. She sits in the leather chair and faces the audience.]

EB: Please join me in welcoming my guest today, the great Sir Isaac Newton.

[Audience claps and cheers as Sir Isaac Newton (IN) shuffles in and sits down next to EB. EB turns to face IN.] 5

Now, I have lots of questions for you but the first question has to be this: we all know that you are a genius but were you born a genius or did you learn how to become one?

[IN takes off his thick-rimmed glasses and starts to clean them with his handkerchief. He looks embarrassed.] 10

IN: You flatter me but no, I certainly wasn't born with any particularly special skills or ability. In fact, I was so weak and small when I was born that I wasn't expected to live.

EB: When and where were you born?

IN: I was born in 1642 in Lincolnshire, not far from Grantham. 15

EB: Do you come from a long line of great scholars?

IN: No, not at all. One of my uncles was a clergyman and he gave me a book about logic when I was at Cambridge, which I enjoyed reading very much, but other than that, no. My father made a simple living farming his own land but unfortunately he died before I was born. 20

EB: So was it just you and your mother at home?

IN: No, my mother remarried the Reverend Barnabas Smith, although he sadly passed away when I was 14. I spent much of my youth with my mother's mother. She was a wonderful lady who I loved very much and we were very happy living in the family home until it was time for me to go to school. 25

EB: What was your school like?

IN: I was sent to Grantham Grammar School where I quickly became bottom of the class in every subject.

EB: You were bottom of the class? I find that hard to believe!

IN: No, it's true. I only took an interest in my school work after I had been in a fight. That fight changed my life. 30

EB: What happened?

IN: There was a boy in my class who was always top at everything. One day he persisted in winding me up; telling me I was stupid and that I couldn't do anything. I was sick of him telling everyone that I was useless. I had finally 35 reached the end of my tether, so I punched him in the stomach and then on his arms and his nose. He tried to hit back but I was so enraged that I didn't give him a chance. He lay on the floor with a bloodied nose and bruised cheek, while I stood up free of any cuts or bruises. I was suddenly hailed a champion by my classmates! *(Mutterings of disapproval from the audience)* Thinking back 40 about the fight that evening, I realised that violence was not the way to solve my problems and I felt ashamed at my actions. Instead, I decided to prove this boy wrong once and for all by beating him academically. From that moment on I studied hard and, before the end of that school year, I was top in nearly every subject. (*Audience claps and IN looks victorious*) 45

EB: It sounds as if that boy was pivotal in your life.

IN: Yes, he was. I continued to read more and study more. In fact, I improved so much that I won the school shield.

EB: So, after school you went straight to Cambridge then?

IN: No I didn't go straight there. My mother decided that I would do better to follow 50 in my father's footsteps. I agreed, as I felt that he would have been proud of me taking after him and running the farm. I mean, the house and farmland had been in our family for over a hundred years and I didn't want to let my family down.

EB: So you became a farmer then?

IN: Well, I tried to. I became an apprentice to get some hands-on experience 55 but, in all honesty, I frequently forgot where I was meant to be and what I was meant to be doing, preferring instead to wander off with my nose stuck in a book. In the end, my mother decided that perhaps Cambridge was better for me, so that was where I was sent.

EB: I bet you flourished at university? 60

IN: No, not at all. In fact for the first two years I did very little other than what I needed to do to pass my classes. I spent most of my time pursuing my hobbies instead.

EB: Now then, I've heard a lot about your hobbies and interests. Didn't you make sundials? 65

IN: For as long as I can remember I have always been interested in making things. I love making things with my hands: sundials, kites, paper lanterns, models and buildings, for example. I like to think with my brain and then create with my fingers.

EB: Is this what you did at college? 70

IN: No, at Cambridge I was trying to work out the force of wind using a scale that I had made. I thought that if I jumped with the wind and recorded how far I had jumped, it would give me a model that I could use to record wind force. Now I know that sounds primitive but it did work and I was sure that this could be used to create a wind force gauge. 75

EB: So did you get your degree?

IN: Yes. I got my BA degree when I was 22 and was about to gain my MA degree when, of course, the Great Plague broke out in London and everyone at college was sent back home lest we should catch that dreadful, deadly disease. Fortunately we were unaffected in Grantham, but many of the boys 80 from the London area caught the Plague and many died. It was so very sad but that really gave me the push to do something meaningful.

[*IN runs his hands through his thick, grey hair and scratches his head. He sighs deeply and looks down as a mark of respect.*]

EB: What happened next? 85

IN: Well, funnily enough, during this vacation I found myself sitting under one of our apple trees in the garden. I had been thinking about the force of wind and other forces of nature when an apple fell down. I looked up into the tree at the apples that were hanging there and I thought, 'Why don't they all fall down?' Of course, I finally realised that they only fall when the weight and size is right for the gravitational pull to force them down off the tree. *90*

EB: What is gravitational pull?

IN: Well, gravity is the natural force that keeps us on the ground. If it wasn't for gravity we would all float upwards. Gravity pulls downwards. In the example of the apple on the tree, the weight of the fruit becomes too heavy for the tree to *95* hold on to it because the force of gravity is too powerful. This causes the apple to drop.

EB: So gravity is an unseen force that just pushes and pulls everything downwards?

IN: No! Gravity is a force that only pulls, not pushes. Once I had made this discovery, it was so exciting to write down my theories. Of course, since then *100* so many other scholars have written papers and have completed research on the subject of gravity.

EB: Now that you have worked on gravity you must find yourself feeling quite bored and have little else to do.

[IN sits back in his chair and chuckles, revealing suit arms that are far too short and *105* *a shirt that is not tucked into his trousers.]*

IN: Ah, you don't know me! I'm even busier than usual, working on my theories of light and optics. There is so much to study and so little time to study it that I never get a moment's rest! Do you know that my mind is so full of facts and figures that I frequently forget to eat or even get dressed properly! Only *110* last week I was walking into the village before I realised that I didn't have any clothes on! (*Audience laughs and IN looks shy*)

EB: (*EB turns to face the audience*) Now, is that the mark of a true genius or what, ladies and gentleman? Well, we shall have to leave it there as time is sadly running out. Please join me in thanking our guest, Sir Isaac Newton. *115* (*Thunderous applause from the audience and from EB as IN smiles politely. EB turns back to IN.*) We look forward to hearing more about your theories of light and optics.

Original text by Michellejoy Hughes

1 What reason did Newton give for not being born a genius?

B 2

1

_____

2 Explain, in your own words, what inspired Newton to progress to the top of his class.

B 2

_____

_____

_____

_____

3

_____

3 Newton flourished as a farmer. Do you agree with this statement? Support your answer with THREE pieces of evidence.

B 2

_____

_____

_____

_____

○ 3

4 Which sentence tells us that Newton enjoyed designing and then creating what he had designed?

B 2

_____

○ 1

5 In which year did Newton receive his first degree?

B 2

_____

○ 1

6 Tick the TWO statements that are true.

B 2

A Newton's step-father was a farmer. ☐

B Newton was raised by his grandmother. ☐

C The farm had been in the family for over a century. ☐

D The Great Plague killed many boys in Grantham. ☐

E Newton started to think about gravity while sat under a pear tree. ☐

○ 2

7 What do you think each of these phrases means?

B 2

a '... I had finally reached the end of my tether...' (lines 35–36)

_____

_____

b '... to follow in my father's footsteps' (lines 50–51)

_____

_____

c '... to wander off with my nose stuck in a book' (lines 57–58)

_____

_____

○ 3

8 Give an alternative word that could replace each of these words as they are used in the text.

   a primitive (line 74) _____   **b** scholars (line 16) _____

   c pursuing (line 62) _____   **d** persisted (line 34) _____

9 How did the wind scale work? Refer to the text in your answer.

_____

_____

_____

10 Which event encouraged Newton to do something significant with his life?

_____

_____

11 How does Newton describe gravity?

_____

12 Give a physical description of Newton. Use the text to support your answer.

_____

_____

_____

_____

13 What type of source do you think this extract has been taken from? Find SIX pieces of evidence to support your answer.

_____

_____

_____

_____

_____

_____

_____

FROM the city of Calais, on the northern coast of France, one may look over the
water on a clear day and see the white cliffs of Dover, in England. At this point
the English Channel is only twenty-one miles wide. But this narrow water has
dangerous currents, and often fierce winds sweep over it, so that small ships find
it hard to cross. This rough Channel has more than once spoiled the plans of   5
England's enemies, and the English people have many times thanked God for their
protecting seas.

Indeed, the British Isles belong more to the sea than to the land. They once
formed a peninsula, jutting out from Europe, far into the Atlantic Ocean; and thus
they remained for countless ages. But a long struggle for mastery went on between   10
sea and land. It ended at last, ages before our story begins, by the sinking of the
land between England and France, and between Scotland and Norway. The rolling,
tireless sea poured over these low places, to form the North Sea and the English
Channel. The Irish Sea and St. George's Channel were formed in the same manner.
The result is that we now have the two islands of Great Britain and Ireland, with   15
a number of smaller ones belonging to the same group, instead of that long-ago
peninsula of the Continent of Europe.

The sea took the people of these islands for its own. It shut them off from their
enemies in the early days of their weakness. It gave them plenty of warm rains, which
makes grass and grain grow green and tall. It gave them abundance of fish for food;   20
and when they became stronger as a people, it furnished them with broad highways
by which they might trade with other nations. So the people of Great Britain have put
their trust in the sea, looking to it for their wealth and their strength. ...

But Great Britain has many advantages besides the sea, else it would be no
better off than many other islands.   25

First, its climate is excellent, neither very cold in winter nor very warm in summer.
... The reason is that along the western coasts of Ireland and Scotland runs the
warm Gulf Stream.

There are many rivers, some of them broad and deep, up which ships may go
for a considerable distance into the land. The chief of these are the Thames, the   30
Severn, the Mersey, and the Clyde. Besides the river mouths, the country has an
irregular coast on all sides, forming many sheltered harbours for ships.

Again, there is a goodly amount of very fertile soil, capable of raising nearly every
crop that can be grown in any part of the temperate zone. Then, too, there is great
wealth of minerals in the depths of the earth – tin in the southwest of England, and 35
coal and iron in the north and west.

Where there are mines there are usually mountains. So it is in Great Britain. Along the western side of the island the country is mountainous, especially in the extreme west, which is called Wales. The loftiest mountain here is Mount Snowdon, which is about 3500 feet high. In the northern part is Scotland, where the mountains are quite rugged. Wales and northern Scotland are the wilder parts of the island, and were the parts which the English were longest in getting into their possession.

Great Britain is a goodly country – good for man, and beast. It was good for savage men; it was good for men who were beginning to advance beyond savages; and it is good now for a great and powerful nation.

The earliest people of Great Britain, like those of other parts of the world, were savages, who lived in caves or flimsy huts, and had only the rudest weapons. They are called 'stone men', because they clipped stones into shape so as to make rough axes and knives. The later stone men made smooth and polished weapons, similar to the Indian knives and axes which you may see in museums. They had tamed the dog to serve them, and also had oxen, pigs, sheep, and goats.

But, after all, we know very little of these stone men. They disappeared long before civilized men visited these islands, and their place was taken by a people who used 'bronze' weapons, made from a mixture of tin and copper.

These men of the 'bronze age' were the Britons, and from them the island is still called Britain. Like most Europeans, the Britons were men of 'Aryan' speech. The European languages have so many likenesses to one another that scholars think they must all have come from one original tongue. It is supposed that this language was spoken – long before men began to make records of their deeds – by one original nation, living somewhere in western Asia or Eastern Europe; and from it the present European nations are all descended. This supposed original people is called Aryan, and those peoples who speak any language descended from theirs are said to be peoples of Aryan speech. The Celts – that is, the Irish, Welsh, Scots, and ancient Gauls – are one branch of the Aryan peoples. Other branches are: the ancient Greeks and Romans; the Teutons (including the Germans and the Dutch); and the Slavs (Russians, Poles, and Serbians). In Asia, the Persians and the ancient Hindus also spoke Aryan tongues.

Moving forward, step by step, the Celts settled in Western Europe, at some time before history began. The Gauls remained in the country we call France. Others of the Celts, chief among whom were the Britons, moved across the Channel and gave their name to the British Isles.

The Britons were tall and slender, with light complexions and blue eyes. Many of them had red hair. When they went to war they stained their faces and bodies with a bluish dye taken from one of their native herbs. They fought mostly on foot, using swords and spears. They were fierce and bold and ready to resist any invader; but they were not systematic in their fighting, and when steadily attacked would give way. Their bronze weapons and tools were harder and sharper than the stone implements of the earlier peoples. They made small round boats, of basket-work covered with skins. They ploughed the land and raised wheat. They could spin and weave; they knew something of mining and metal-working; they could quarry great stones from the hills; and they exchanged their tin for the goods of Gaul and other countries.

Yet the Britons had no cities or towns, but lived in rude villages. Their huts were round, somewhat like Indian wigwams; they were built of sticks and reeds, though sometimes they had stone foundations.

The Britons believed in many gods. These included one who was supreme over all, besides a sun god, a god of thunder, and others. The worship of the Britons included bloody sacrifices of both animals and men. The human sacrifices were usually of criminals, or of captives taken in war; but sometimes innocent persons were sacrificed to their gods. The priests were called Druids, and they were the most learned men among the Britons. They were respected almost as much as the chiefs and kings, and were consulted on all questions of law and religion.

At several places in England there are still standing some peculiar stone structures, erected in these early days. The most famous of these is Stonehenge, near Salisbury. It is a circle of huge stones set on end, with great stones laid crosswise upon them. Smaller circles and ovals are arranged within the great circle. One of the stones at Stonehenge weighs nearly seventy tons. The whole circle stands in the midst of burial places, and it probably had something to do with the worship of these early peoples.

No one knows how long the Britons were the ruling race in these islands. But whether it was many centuries, or only a few, they did not learn to unite under a single government. They had many chiefs, but none who was recognized throughout the country as supreme.

So, when the Romans made an invasion into their land, no united resistance was possible. The stricter discipline and firmer organization of the Romans won the victory, and Britain was added to the great Empire of Rome.

From *The Story of England* by Samuel B. Harding

1 How far is England from France?

_____

2 Give TWO reasons why the Channel can be difficult to navigate.

_____

_____

3 Explain, in your own words, how the United Kingdom was physically formed.

_____

_____

_____

_____

4 What do you think is meant by the sentence, 'But a long struggle for mastery went on between sea and land' (lines 10–11)?

_____

_____

_____

5 Which FOUR benefits did the sea provide for the early inhabitants of Great Britain?

_____

_____

_____

_____

6 Complete each sentence using ONE word from those listed below.

tin   coal   minerals   bronze   stone

Celts   Teutons   Slavs   Persia   Gauls

a In the north of England there are mines of _____.

b The Dutch people were classed as _____.

c The people from Scotland are classed as _____.

d The most durable tools were made of _____.

7 Which ONE word describes the land to the far west of Great Britain?

_____

8 Where did the Aryan people live?

_____

_____

9 Imagine that you are fighting the Britons and one of them is coming towards you, ready to attack. Using the text to help you, describe, in your own words, what the Briton looks like.

_____

_____

_____

_____

_____

_____

10 Tick the TWO statements that are false.

B 2

A The Britons believed in more than one god. ☐

B Great Britain takes its name from its early inhabitants. ☐

C The Britons traded their tin with France. ☐

D Mount Snowdon is the second highest mountain in Wales. ☐

E The Britons built their homes mostly out of stones. ☐

2

11 What does the reader learn from the text about the Druids? Refer to FOUR pieces of evidence in your answer.

B 2

_____

_____

_____

_____

_____

4

12 Why do you think that Stonehenge was built? Refer to the text in your answer.

B 2

_____

_____

1

13 Give THREE reasons that explain why the Romans were able to conquer Britain.

B 2

_____

_____

_____

_____

3

Now go to the Progress Chart to record your score!   Total   35

B 1

'Twas the night before Christmas, when all through the house
Not a creature was stirring, not even a mouse.
The stockings were hung by the chimney with care,
In hopes that St Nicholas soon would be there.

The children were nestled all snug in their beds,   5
While visions of sugar-plums danced in their heads.
And mamma in her 'kerchief, and I in my cap,
Had just settled our brains for a long winter's nap.

When out on the lawn there arose such a clatter,
I sprang from the bed to see what was the matter.   10
Away to the window I flew like a flash,
Tore open the shutters and threw up the sash.

The moon on the breast of the new-fallen snow
Gave the lustre of mid-day to objects below.
When, what to my wondering eyes should appear,   15
But a miniature sleigh, and eight tiny reindeer.

With a little old driver, so lively and quick,
I knew in a moment it must be St Nick.
More rapid than eagles his coursers they came,
And he whistled, and shouted, and called them by name!   20

"Now Dasher! now, Dancer! now, Prancer and Vixen!
On, Comet! On, Cupid! On, Donder and Blitzen!
To the top of the porch! to the top of the wall!
Now dash away! dash away! dash away all!"

As dry leaves that before the wild hurricane fly,   25
When they meet with an obstacle, mount to the sky.
So up to the house-top the coursers they flew,
With the sleigh full of Toys, and St Nicholas too.

And then, in a twinkling, I heard on the roof
The prancing and pawing of each little hoof.   30
As I drew in my head, and was turning around,
Down the chimney St Nicholas came with a bound.

He was dressed all in fur, from his head to his foot,
And his clothes were all tarnished with ashes and soot.
A bundle of Toys he had flung on his back,   35
And he looked like a peddler, just opening his pack.

His eyes – how they twinkled! his dimples how merry!
His cheeks were like roses, his nose like a cherry!
His droll little mouth was drawn up like a bow,
And the beard of his chin was as white as the snow.   40

The stump of a pipe he held tight in his teeth,
And the smoke it encircled his head like a wreath.
He had a broad face and a little round belly,
That shook when he laughed, like a bowlful of jelly!

He was chubby and plump, a right jolly old elf,   45
And I laughed when I saw him, in spite of myself!
A wink of his eye and a twist of his head,
Soon gave me to know I had nothing to dread.

He spoke not a word, but went straight to his work,
And filled all the stockings, then turned with a jerk,   50
And laying his finger aside of his nose,
And giving a nod, up the chimney he rose!

He sprang to his sleigh, to his team gave a whistle,
And away they all flew like the down of a thistle.
But I heard him exclaim, 'ere he drove out of sight,   55
"Happy Christmas to all, and to all a good-night!"

'Twas the Night before Christmas by Clement Clarke Moore

1 What was the date on the night that a clatter was heard outside?

_____

B 2
1

2 How does the reader know that the children were asleep? Refer to the text in your answer.

_____

_____

B 2
1

3 Who is narrating the tale?

_____

B 2
1

4 Was it noisy in the **narrator's** house before St Nicholas arrived? Explain your answer with reference to the text.

_____

_____

B 2
2

5 Give TWO reasons that explain why it was as light as day outside.

_____

_____

B 2
2

6 What do you think a 'sash' is (line 12)?

_____

_____

B 2
1

7 Find ONE **simile** in each of the sections of text shown below.

   a lines 37–40 _____

   b lines 41–44 _____

   c lines 53–56 _____

B 2
3

8 What do you think each phrase means?

   a '… my wondering eyes …' (line 15)

_____

_____

   b '… in a twinkling …' (line 29)

_____

_____

B 2
2

9 Which phrase describes the speed of the reindeer?

B 2

1

_____

10 If the names of the reindeer were put in alphabetical order, which one would come fourth?

B 2

1

_____

11 How did the **narrator** know not to be scared when St Nicholas came into the room? Refer to the text in your answer.

B 2

_____

_____

2

12 Describe, in your own words, what St Nick looked like. Your answer should refer to SIXTEEN pieces of evidence.

B 2

_____

_____

_____

_____

_____

_____

_____

_____

_____

_____

_____

_____

8

13 Give an alternative word that could replace each of these words as used in the text.

B 2

a brains (line 8) _____

b tarnished (line 34) _____

c bundle (line 35) _____

3

14 Find TWO **homophones** in this sentence. Write them, with their **homophone** partners, below.

B 2

'I knew in a moment it must be St Nick.'

_____ / _____

_____ / _____

2

15 How is the reader made to feel that St Nicholas is a happy person? Support your answer with FIVE pieces of evidence.

B 2

_____

_____

_____

_____

_____

_____

_____

5

Progress Chart   Third papers in Comprehension

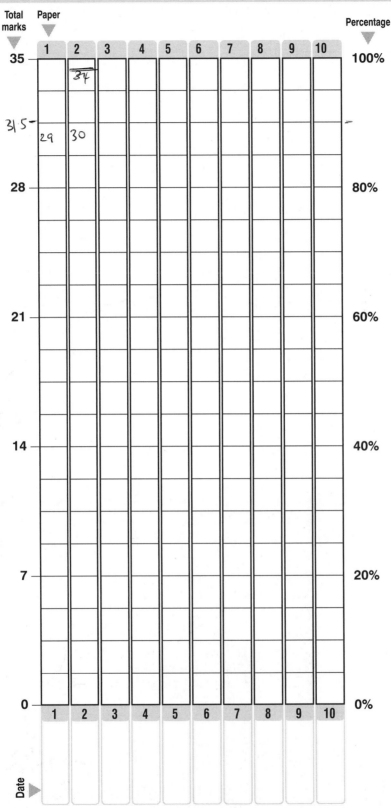

When you've finished the book use the Next Steps Planner